Temptation

or

Virtue Rewarded

A melodrama

Winifred Phelps

Samuel French — London
New York — Toronto — Hollywood

ISBN 0 573 02265 8

Please see page iv for further copyright information

CHARACTERS

(in the order of their appearance)

LADY LUCRE
ARABELLA, her daughter
CLARENCE
SIR JASPER BREAKNECK
FANNY

SYNPOSIS OF SCENES

TEMPTATION SORDID or VIRTUE REWARDED

When the LIGHTS *come up the* CHAIRMAN *is seated at a table or desk* L *of the proscenium arch and outside the picture. From here his lines may be spoken or read.*

CHAIRMAN. And now, ladies and gentlemen, we have obtained, at enormous expense, the services of this magnificent company of players who will now present to you the story of love, courage and faith triumphant entitled *Temptation Sordid* or *Virtue Rewarded* by Winifred Phelps. The characters in this gripping melodrama are: Lady Lucre, played by . . . (*here insert the name of the actress playing the part*), her sweet daughter, Arabella, played by . . . , Sir Jasper Breakneck, Arabella's first cousin once removed and twice convicted, by . . . , our hero, Clarence Whiteheart, by . . . , and Fanny, a lady of questionable morals but of undoubted charm by . . . The whole production is in the very capable hands of . . . (*here he quotes the name of the producer*)

SCENE I

SCENE—*A room in Lucre Hall. There is a table down* R *with an upright chair* R *of it. On the table are numerous samples of Lady Lucre's jewels.*

When the CURTAIN *rises* LADY LUCRE *is seated at the table engaged in the empty but absorbing occupation of trying on her jewellery.*

LADY LUCRE. Ah me, life is very dull for me since my dear husband passed away! (*She weeps*) There is nothing in this weary world for me to do, but to try on me jools! If only me pretty daughter, Arabella, could find a husband worthy of her! Then, perhaps, I could have some little grandchildren to play about my feet! What a joy that would be! But alas, she is so young and innocent! She should not yet be exposed to the horrors of married life—to the perfidy of men in general and of husbands in particular! Of course, Sir Jasper, her first cousin once removed and twice convicted *would* marry her, but I fear it would only be for her money and not for her pretty face and sweet nature! Ah me, so much wealth is a burden and not a pleasure—although I must admit I do enjoy trying on me jools! Arabella, bring me some more diamonds!

(ARABELLA *enters* R *with a jewel box or bowl of diamonds, etc., and stands* L *of the table*)

ARABELLA. Here, Mother dear. These will help you to pass the tedious hours. (*Aside*) What a dreary life mother leads now father is dead! Nothing to do all day but to try on her diamonds! Perhaps if I tell her about dear Clarence, it will add a little interest to her weary life! (*To her mother*) Mother dear, I have a friend outside who wishes to speak with you!

LADY LUCRE. Yes, dear. Who is she?

ARABELLA. It isn't a she. It's a he, Mother dear.

LADY LUCRE. But, my dear, you don't know any hes! You are only eighteen and are not yet old enough to have known any hes—except, of course, Sir Jasper, your first cousin once removed and twice convicted.

ARABELLA. Oh, Mother, do not speak of that odious man in the same breath as my dear Clarence! (*Soulfully*) He is so good-looking, and upright! He comes of such an excellent family. His father is a clergyman of good repute— (*ecstacy dims a little at this point*)—although I fear he married an actress! But Clarence is so kind—he inherits . . .

LADY LUCRE. Yes, dear child?

ARABELLA. He inherits all his father's saintly attributes, and he wishes to speak with you to ask for my hand in marriage!

LADY LUCRE. Oh, he does, does he! And where, may I ask, did you meet him? Arabella, some more diamonds!

(ARABELLA *goes out* R *and returns immediately with some more diamonds*)

ARABELLA (*handing them to her mother*) I was playing croquet with Lady Chatterley's lover-ly daughter in her garden, when the ball went under the gooseberry bush, and he risked his manly beauty on those horrid prickles to get it for me!

LADY LUCRE (*aside*) Obviously a brave young man, if not a wealthy one! Perhaps a more suitable match than Sir Jasper, her first cousin once removed and twice convicted! Daughter, bring him to me!

ARABELLA (*calling as she moves off L*) Clarence! Clarence!

(ARABELLA *goes off* L. *She returns immediately, followed by* CLARENCE)

CLARENCE. And now, my love, introduce me to your mother that I may ask for your hand! (*He kisses her hand*) The dearest little hand in all the world, if I may say so!

ARABELLA (*coyly*) Oh, Clarence! Mother dear, this is Clarence of whom I spoke!

LADY LUCRE. Ah, so you are the young gallant who risked life and limb to rescue a croquet ball from under the gooseberry bush?

CLARENCE. Madame, I would risk more than that for the sake of your dear daughter!

LADY LUCRE. I understand that you wish to ask for the hand of my daughter in marriage?

CLARENCE. To receive your permission to marry your daughter would make me the happiest man in England! But I must be honest and tell you that I can offer her nothing but my love, clean hands and a clean heart! Of wealth, I have none!

LADY LUCRE. Arabella, pass me some more diamonds!

(ARABELLA *goes out* R *and brings in some more diamonds. She returns and stands holding them during the ensuing speech*)

So, young man, you come here to take from me the joy of my life—my little flower, Arabella—the little flower who has been nurtured in a hothouse with every comfort that money can buy! And you have nothing to offer—nothing with which to maintain the standards of luxury to which she was born! Why, Sir Jasper, her first cousin once removed and twice convicted has more than that—at least he has a small Post Office savings account!

ARABELLA (*putting the diamonds on the table*) But, Mother, I do not *love* Sir Jasper!

(SIR JASPER *enters down* L)

SIR JASPER. What is this I hear? That my little cousin does not love me? Fie upon you! And who is this charming young man? (*Aside*) As if I didn't know—the young upstart!

LADY LUCRE. This, Sir Jasper, is young Clarence Something-or-other. And this, young man, is Arabella's kinsman, Sir Jasper Breakneck, her first cousin once removed and twice convicted!

(SIR JASPER *and* CLARENCE *bow distantly to one another*)

SIR JASPER. And who, young man, may you be?

CLARENCE. Oi be—er—I am Clarence Whiteheart, in love with this fair flower, Arabella. But alas, I can offer her nothing but my love, clean hands and a clean heart!

SIR JASPER. And what does our fair cousin say?

ARABELLA. I love him dearly, however poor he be!

SIR JASPER (*over the footlights*) How naïve she is! I must woo her and dazzle her with me charm! The old girl's wealth is almost worth working for! (*To Arabella*) How laudable the sentiment! But from my position, as a man of the world, I suggest you wait here for him, whilst he sails away to seek his fortune! I will stay here and care for you—with brotherly affection, of course, my dear cousin—until his return!

CLARENCE. An excellent idea! (*To Lady Lucre*) But how shall I know, dear lady, that in my absence, this delicate flower may not be picked by some other hand?

ARABELLA (*soulfully*) Rest assured, dearest. I shall be here when you return! You shall be in my thoughts all day and in my dreams each night!

CLARENCE. Farewell, I go to seek my fortune, and when I return with it, you will see I still have clean hands and a clean heart! At least I will have left something of myself with you——

LADY LUCRE. Clarence!!

Clarence. —part of my heart is ever in your keeping, Arabella dearest!

(*They embrace*)

And now, away—to America, fame and fortune!

(*With a magnificent gesture,* Clarence *exits* L *whilst*

Arabella *collapses in floods of tears at Lady Lucre's feet*)

Sir Jasper (*over the footlights*) Ha, ha, now I have me chance! But wait, what is best to do? To stay here and woo me fair cousin in his absence, or to follow him, in the guise of a friend, steal his fortune, after he has made it, dispose of him—(*much hand-rubbing*) and come back here to claim my bride and a further fortune! Yes, so be it! I will away whilst they commune together. Farewell! Ha, ha!

Sir Jasper *exits* L.
Lady Lucre *and* Arabella *exit* R *as—*

the Lights *are dimmed*

Chairman. And so we leave our heroine in tears, to follow Clarence who goes to seek his fortune, little knowing that the dastardly Sir Jasper is up to his usual dirty tricks. The next scene takes place on board ship the following day as our hero sails towards America.

SCENE II

Scene—*On board ship bound for America. The small table and chair are hidden behind a screen for this scene and the long table is upended parallel with the footlights to represent the deck of a ship.*

When the Lights *come up* Sir Jasper *is seen, with a telescope under his arm, pacing the boatdeck. He stops and focuses his telescope off* L *before he speaks. The characters in this scene should try to sway with the boat's action, so to speak. Any diversity of direction will probably only cause more amusement from the audience.*

Sir Jasper. I can see that young Clarence is aboard.

Methinks that if I pace the deck here for a short time, he will soon pass by and then I will get into conversation with him. Ah, but here comes our hero—quick, me disguise! (*He affects disguise*) Gadzooks, but this boat's pitching and tossing a lot!

(CLARENCE *enters* L *dressed exactly as before, complete with white gloves to ensure those "clean hands"*)

(*In an "old man's" voice*) Good evening, young man, could you spare a lonely old man a few minutes' chat, to help pass the long hours of our hazardous journey?

CLARENCE (*over the footlights*) What a feeble old gentleman! A kind word never comes amiss! (*To Sir Jasper*) Certainly, sir, it will be a pleasure!

SIR JASPER. Why are you travelling to America, my young friend?

CLARENCE. To seek my fortune, sir. The fair young lady who promises to be my wife is awaiting my return in England, and it is my earnest wish to lay that fortune at her feet!

SIR JASPER. Rightly said, young man. And what do you seek—gold?—diamonds?—oil?

CLARENCE (*thoughtfully*) I don't really know which to choose! What do you, kind sir, out of the experience of your many years, suggest?

SIR JASPER. Young man, what are diamonds, but glass? (*Aside*) The old girl's got enough of those, which Arabella will inherit and which will ultimately come to me! (*To Clarence*) Oil? A bit messy, don't you think? And you can't carry much of it back with you! But gold—(*with much sniggering and hand-rubbing*)—now, that's nice—done up in handy brick-size—easy to carry—(*aside*) and easy for me to bring home when I have disposed of him! (*To Clarence*) Young man, I say gold!

CLARENCE. Gold it shall be! Old gentleman, you have been so kind! Would that we were travelling together, so that I might have the benefit of your experience, whilst in that vast America!

SIR JASPER. I am full of years! Not much time remains to me! If that time can be spent serving youth, I shall die a happy man! (*Aside*) Fool! He's playing right into me hands! (*To Clarence*) Let me travel with you! I fear my infirmity will not allow me to work hard—but if we were to live together, perhaps I could get your tea for you sometimes?

CLARENCE. Oh, Heaven reward you for your great kindness! With my youth and your experience, we should make a wonderful partnership—but stay!

(*A strong light is seen to be flashing from down* R)

What is that blinking light over yonder?

SIR JASPER (*inspecting it thoroughly with his telescope*) It is the Nantucket Lightship! We have arrived in America! Strange how interesting conversation can shorten the longest journey!

CLARENCE. Come, old gentleman, here is my arm! Let us face the future and Dame Fortune together with a smile!

SIR JASPER (*over the footlights*) He'll smile on the other side of his face soon! Coming, dear boy, coming!

(SIR JASPER *goes to* CLARENCE, *takes his arm and they totter off* R. *The* LIGHTS *are lowered and the* CHAIRMAN *takes up the story*)

CHAIRMAN. And so we see how the kindly, guileless youth was taken in by the dastardly Sir Jasper. Time passes as they make their weary way across America to wherever it is that gold is found. And they set up home and Clarence spends his days seeking the elusive gold whilst Sir Jasper spends *his* days hatching up more plots! Our next scene takes place in the bar-room of a low-down hostelry in a gold-mining town, and if there are any children here under the age of two, the management suggests they be taken out of the hall immediately, as it is at this point that Temptation rears its ugly head!

SCENE III

SCENE—*The bar-room of a low-down hostelry in a gold-mining town somewhere in America. The long table is now set diagonally across the stage down* L *to represent the bar.*

When the LIGHTS *come up a local lady called* FANNY *is sitting on the downstage end of the bar, crosslegged and with as much leg and garter showing as possible.*

FANNY (*chewing very obviously*) Gosh, it's quiet in the little ol' town tonight. Ain't nuthin' goin' to happen nohow?

(CLARENCE *enters* R, *still immaculately dressed plus white gloves*)

CLARENCE. Good evening, madame! (*He sees her garter*) Oh, excuse me! (*Aside*) I must control myself! I told my dearest I would return to her with clean hands and a clean heart!

FANNY. Sorry, big boy, if the sight of a leg unsettles you! I suggest you need something to remedy that!

CLARENCE. Please don't be suggestive! The lowering of your skirt to reasonable dimensions is all that is necessary!

FANNY. O.K. then, big boy, come over and lower it!

(CLARENCE, *with eyes averted or covered, diffidently approaches as though the garter may well bite him, and makes a convulsive grab at the skirt, thus bringing it down to respectability*)

Now cut out the rough stuff, big boy! (*Over the footlights*) What a prig! I'll teach him a thing or two! (*She leans over to get a bottle of whisky and two glasses*) Come along over here, big boy! Let's fill 'em up!

CLARENCE. No liquor shall touch my lips whilst I am away from my beloved! A glass of milk, please!

FANNY. A glass of what? Did you say a glass of milk? Say, do you think we have any cows around here?

CLARENCE. In that case, give me a glass of Nature's wine! Water shall be my portion!

FANNY. Aw, for cryin' out loud! If you need it that bad, I think we may have one! (*She leans over and finds a glass of milk, but pours out a glass of whisky for herself*)

CLARENCE. Your very good health, madame!

FANNY (*over the footlights*) Say, who does he think I am? Ah, well, I'd better be nice to him—it's all good for trade!

(*They drink to each other and* FANNY *tries to put her arms around his neck*)

And what are you doing so far from home, my little chicka-dee?

CLARENCE. I've come with an old friend who keeps house for me, to seek gold!

FANNY. Sure, sure, plenty of suckers do that but precious few succeed!

CLARENCE. Never fear, I shall! (*He raises his hat*) I shall, no doubt, be in each evening for my glass of milk until such a time as I find my fortune and return to my true love! Farewell!

FANNY (*aside*) If you find your fortune, I'll see you don't return to your true love, whomever she be! (*To Clarence*) O.K., kiddo, be seein' you!

(CLARENCE *exits* R. *A quick* BLACK-OUT *follows*)

CHAIRMAN. And so time passed. Hard-working day suc-ceeded hard-working day until one evening, Clarence comes staggering in . . .

(*The* LIGHTS *come up*)

CLARENCE (*off*) Fanny, Fanny, look what I've found!

(CLARENCE *comes staggering in* R, *carrying several gold bricks which he places on the bar, upon which* FANNY *is seated in her usual place and fashion.* FANNY *turns in a bored fashion, but leaps down when she sees what he has brought*)

FANNY. Say, big boy, you sure struck it rich! What are those supposed to be?

CLARENCE. Gold bricks, Fanny! And I have some more without, which I couldn't carry! Look after these, my dear, whilst I bring them in!

(CLARENCE *exits* R *whilst* FANNY *carefully examines the bricks, testing them with her teeth.*
CLARENCE *enters* R)

FANNY (*as Clarence returns*) Oh, how wonderful, Clarence, you came for gold and you found it! (*Darting from side to side to see whether anyone has overheard*) But careful, Clarence, there are bad men in the town and these lovely bricks should be guarded night and day!

CLARENCE. My old friend, Honest John, will guard them with his life!

FANNY. I do not trust him! Let me help you! Take me home with you! And when you retire at night to your humble room—with these lovely bricks stacked in the corner—let me be there with you! I will watch over them —and you—like a mother watching her children! (*Over the footlights*) And if he swallows that one, he'll swallow anything!

CLARENCE. But how can I allow a poor weak woman to do this for me?

FANNY. Think nothing of it, my dear Clarence! Before I came out here, I was a children's nurse, and I spent many happy hours watching my charges as they slept—God bless their little souls! How happy I shall be to spend the night in your room—watching those lovely bricks! Think of me as Fanny the Nanny!

CLARENCE (*aside*) Oh, Arabella, trust me! All this shall be done with your well-being in mind! (*To Fanny*) My good friend, I accept your generous offer in the spirit in which it was made! Let us away to meet my old friend, Honest John! How he will rejoice in my good fortune! Come on, Nanny!

(CLARENCE *and* FANNY *exit* R *as the* LIGHTS *are lowered and the* CHAIRMAN *takes up the tale*)

CHAIRMAN. And so Clarence and Fanny go home, laden with the gold. And in our next scene, we see them and Sir Jasper coming aboard ship with the gold bricks for the journey home. We will not enquire what Fanny and Sir Jasper have been doing since she came to live with Clarence and with Sir Jasper. Little does poor Clarence know that they have plotted together to steal the gold. But, quiet! If we listen, perhaps we can hear what further villainy they are cooking up!

SCENE IV

SCENE—*On board ship. The same setting as in Scene II.*

When the LIGHTS *come up* SIR JASPER *enters* R *followed by* FANNY.
They are staggering under the weight of the gold bricks.

SIR JASPER. Aboard at last—and the gold is in our care!
Can we find some way to make Clarence miss the boat and
so keep it all for ourselves? Fanny-me-love, with this in my
possession, I could find you a nice little flat in Town and
we could live on this haul for some time!

(*Over the footlights*)

Once we get to London, I'll give her the slip and keep all
this lovely stuff for myself!

FANNY. Oh, we'll see about the flat later! He *was* paying
off the cab. (*She looks* R) Oh, quick, he's coming! Think
quickly, Jasper—what can we do to keep this for ourselves?
(*Over the footlights*) Once I get to London, I'll give him the
slip and keep all this lovely stuff for myself!

(CLARENCE *enters* R)

CLARENCE. Ah, my friends, my true and honest friends!
And now we are on our way to England, home, and my
true love! (*He steps* R *and with a broad gesture calls*) Cast off!

(*Whereupon they all stagger and then develop a gentle sway as
previously*)

Soon I must say farewell to you both—you who have helped
me to find my fortune and who have guarded it with your
lives! Such devotion—such selflessness demands more than
I can give! And since I have nothing that I *can* give—save
this precious gold, which is for my dearest Arabella—I will
merely give you my hand and raise my hat to you and
say——

(*A strong light is seen to be flashing down* L)

—what is that blinking light over yonder? (*He points* L)
SIR JASPER (*using his telescope*) Ah, the Eddystone light-

house! We are nearly home! Strange how interesting conversation can shorten the longest journeys!

CLARENCE. I had hoped to bother you no further, but since we have arrived so soon—would you both be so good as to help me carry the gold ashore?

SIR JASPER ⎫ (*together*) Delighted, dear boy! (*Over the*
FANNY ⎬ *footlights*) We're not letting him get away
    ⎭ with this little lot!

CLARENCE. Come—my heart yearns for the sight of my dear Arabella! Let us away!

(CLARENCE *exits* L *empty-handed and* SIR JASPER *and* FANNY *stagger after him with the gold as the* LIGHTS *are lowered and the* CHAIRMAN *again takes up the story*)

CHAIRMAN. And now our scene changes again, and we are back again at Lucre Hall, the home of Lady Lucre and her lovely daughter, Arabella. With the impetuosity of youth, Arabella impatiently awaits the arrival home of our hero, Clarence Whiteheart, but Lady Lucre is busily engaged, as before, in trying on her jools! But let us gather around and hear what those two lovely ladies are saying!

SCENE V

SCENE—*A room at Lucre Hall. The same setting as Scene I.*

When the LIGHTS *come up the long table is concealed behind the screen and the small table and chair are again set down* R *and* LADY LUCRE *is once more seated at the table counting her jewels and trying them on.* ARABELLA *is standing near her.*

LADY LUCRE. How impatient you are! Have you nothing to do, child? My old hands are always busy! Bring a chair, child, and join me as I count me jools!

ARABELLA. Mother dear, at forty, I know that Life for you is over, but for me, it should hold much more! How I long to see dear Clarence again! Do you think, Mother dear, that he will remember me? Perhaps he has met someone lovelier than me and they may seek their happiness together, leaving me to become a heart-broken old maid! Oh, Mother, I cannot wait much longer!

LADY LUCRE. Tush, child, such foolishness! It is not so *v*ery long ago that Clarence left you, and no doubt, he will soon be back! I cannot understand, however, why Sir Jasper, your first cousin once removed and twice convicted, has not visited us. If I mistake not, he promised Clarence that he would look after you!

ARABELLA. Oh, Mother, how glad I am that that odious man has not been here! I fear his intentions are not strictly honourable!

LADY LUCRE. Child, what a thing to say! The Breaknecks have always been an honourable family!

ARABELLA. Then, why, Mother, was he once removed and twice convicted?

LADY LUCRE. Such childish prattle!

(*Footsteps are heard off* L. ARABELLA *runs* L *and listens with hand to ear*)

ARABELLA. Hush, Mother—someone is coming! By the manly stride, I would almost think it could be my love! (*Aside*) Be still, my heart, and cease thy frenzied beating! Let me look away and by the time I have counted *ten*, perhaps *he* will be here! One, two—three, four—five, six— seven, eight—nine, ten! (*She counts in twos to allow the audience to chant* "*One, two, Buckle my shoe*") It is he! It is Clarence! But stay—he has an old gentleman with him and a lady— (*aside*) well—perhaps not quite a lady! Oh, Mother, what does this mean? I fear he has found someone who has sup- planted me in his affections!

LADY LUCRE. Come here to me, Arabella! If aught has gone amiss, he shall answer to me also!

(CLARENCE *enters* L *followed by* SIR JASPER *and* FANNY *staggering with the gold as before*)

CLARENCE (*striding over to Arabella*) My love, I come to claim my bride!

ARABELLA. Clarence, I have wearied of waiting! But stay, who is this old gentleman, and who—this—er—lady?

CLARENCE. Dear friends of mine, without whose tender

care, I could not have returned to you with my fortune to claim your hand!

(Sir Jasper *comes forward and places his gold on the table*)

This old man, Honest John, has helped me and has given me the benefit of his vast experience!

Sir Jasper (*over the footlights and moving across to down* l) He does not yet know who I am! Shall I still retain my disguise as Honest John, or shall I tell him who I really am? (*Thoughtfully*) Once the old girl gets her hands on the gold, all is lost! Where is me trusty dagger? (*He draws it from his pocket*) Methinks when next Arabella distracts her mother's attention, I will stab him, make off with the gold, and live the rest of me life in luxury!

Arabella. And the other—er—lady?

Clarence. A lady who, from the purest motives, has done her best to make the hours spent apart from you, a little more pleasant! (*He presents Fanny to Arabella and Lady Lucre*)

(Fanny *puts the gold on the table and come down stage to speak over the footlights. When she has finished, she must remain* r *so that she and Sir Jasper are now ranged one either side of* Clarence, *and near enough to carry out their dastardly schemes*)

Fanny (*over the footlights*) He does not yet know what I'm after! Shall I still retain my pretence of helping him, or shall I tell all? Once the old girl gets her hands on the gold, all is lost! Where is me trusty dagger? (*She draws it from her jewelled garter*) Methinks when next Arabella distracts her mother's attention, I will stab him, make off with the gold, and live the rest of me life in luxury!

Arabella (*turning to her mother*) Mother, I do not understand. She made his life—a little more pleasant?

(On "*She made his life*" Sir Jasper *and* Fanny *quickly raise high their daggers. On "*a little more pleasant?*"* Clarence *stoops down to tie his shoelace, and they lunge forward to stab him, but miss him and stab each other in the heart. They fall one either side of him*)

Clarence (*seeing the two bodies*) Ah me! They are weary from their long journeys! How selfish of me not to have noticed it! But stay, what is this?—Blood? They have killed themselves for love of me! Such devotion! Arabella, turn away! Such a sight is not for eyes such as thine!

ARABELLA. It breaks my heart that you should win my hand and your fortune at such a price! Let me gaze on them in homage! (*Looking down on Fanny, whose fall has revealed her garter*) But stay, this lady is no lady to wear a garter such as this! (*She lightly leaps over Fanny*) And Honest John—so like Sir Jasper, my first cousin once removed and twice convicted! But Heaven preserve us! It *is* my first cousin once removed and twice convicted! (*She lightly leaps back over Fanny*)

LADY LUCRE (*rising*) In that case, take him away, and he shall now be known as your first cousin *twice* removed and twice convicted!

CLARENCE (*striding in a manly fashion across any body which lies in his way*) So now, my love, the future alone lies before us! The past, and all it's—er—debris is behind us!

LADY LUCRE (*inspecting the bodies and seeing the garter*) Ah, now that's a pretty little thing—and well worth adding to my collection! (*She takes the garter off Fanny and holds it up for Arabella to see*) Arabella, some more diamonds!

LADY LUCRE *lifts her skirt in order to put on the garter and it is seen that her downstage leg is covered from knee to ankle with as many jewelled garters as it is possible to wear!*

the CURTAIN *falls*

PRODUCTION NOTES

PLAYING TIME

Approximately twenty-five minutes. As the play was written for audience participation, further time should be allowed for interruptions, etc.

PRODUCTION NOTES

The characters should be played with integrity and absolutely seriously. However foolish the line, the character believes in it implicitly. Our hero, who should speak and make his gestures in an "heroic" fashion is "all white"—so to speak, and our villain is "all black". Following that same analogy, it is clearly seen that Arabella must be pale pink, her illustrious mother, purple, and Fanny, most regretfully, scarlet!! The Chairman, so called because in the original production, he was a Chairman of an Old-Time Music-Hall Bill, of which this melodrama was only one item, may be allowed to read his part and could speak it either from his table at the front of the hall, or from the proscenium arch. Spoken ponderously, his part will allow time for quick limited changes of scene.

N.B. The opening speech of Lady Lucre is the most difficult in the play. It sets the background of the story and of most of the characters, and unless varied in pace and colour, could become a trifle tedious.

STAGING NOTES

The drawing of curtains between the scenes is to be avoided if possible as tension and attention will be broken and will have to be built up afresh each time. Limited changes, in near darkness are possible with limited furniture, including a fourfold screen to cover surplus scenery on stag for any one scene. (*See* diagram opposite)

LIGHTING PLOT

Property fittings required: none
General lighting throughout
At the opening of the Play bring in lighting on the CHAIRMAN's
   table

SCENE I. Interior

Cue 1	At the rise of the CURTAIN *Bring up general lighting*	(Page 1)
Cue 2	LADY LUCRE and ARABELLA exit R *Dim lights to* BLACK-OUT	(Page 5)

SCENE II. Exterior

Cue 3	When furniture is set for Scene 2 *Bring up general lighting*	(Page 5)
Cue 4	CLARENCE: ". . . but stay!" *A strong light flashes down* R	(Page 7)
Cue 5	SIR JASPER and CLARENCE totter off R *Dim lights to* BLACK-OUT	(Page 7)

SCENE III. Interior

Cue 6	When furniture is set for Scene III *Bring up general lighting*	(Page 8)
Cue 7	FANNY: ". . . be seein' you!" CLARENCE *exits* R *Quick* BLACK-OUT	(Page 9)
Cue 8	CHAIRMAN: ". . . comes staggering in . . ." *Bring in general lighting*	(Page 9)

FURNITURE AND PROPERTY PLOT

On stage: Long table, covered on three sides with brown paper
Small table
Upright chair
Fourfold screen

Off stage: 3 boxes of assorted jewellery (ARABELLA)
Tray with bottle of whisky and 2 empty glasses, glass
   of milk, a dagger (FANNY)
Telescope, dagger (SIR JASPER)
6 or 8 gold bricks (CLARENCE)

Personal: CLARENCE: white gloves
SIR JASPER: hat and/or beard for disguise
FANNY: jewelled garter
LADY LUCRE: several jewelled garters

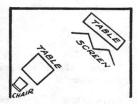

Scenes 1 & 5

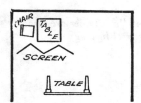

Scenes 2 & 4

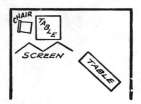

Scene 3

Cue 9   CLARENCE and FANNY exit R   (Page 10)
             Dim lights to BLACK-OUT

SCENE IV.   Exterior

Cue 10   When Scene is reset   (Page 11)
             Bring up general lighting

Cue 11   CLARENCE: "... my hat to vou and say ..."   (Page 11)
             A strong light flashes down L

Cue 12   CLARENCE, SIR JASPER and FANNY exit   (Page 12)
             Dim lights to BLACK-OUT

SCENE V.   Interior

Cue 13   CHAIRMAN: "... ladies are saying!"   (Page 12)
             Bring up general lighting

Men and God

Guy Donegan-Cross

Curate, Christ Church and St Mary's, Old Town, Swindon

GROVE BOOKS LIMITED
RIDLEY HALL RD CAMBRIDGE CB3 9HU

Contents

To John, Hamish and Toby.
Open, vulnerable, loud, crying in public, unashamed to be naked,
at ease with bodily functions, comfortable with women, ready to accept blame,
furious at injustice, learning about God.
4, 2 and 1 years old.
Real men.

The Cover Illustration is by Peter Ashton
and is adapted from da Vinci's "The Anatomy of Man'

First Impression August 2000
ISSN 0262-799X
ISBN 1 85174 439 8

1

Introduction

'I tell you, when women start pissing like us, that's it.'
'Genetic mutations, innit? They're turning into us.'
'A few years and men won't exist, except in a zoo. I mean, we're not needed anymore, are we? Obsolete, dinosaurs, yesterday's news.'

These few lines spoken in a Job Centre in the film *The Full Monty* reverberate with the pain of lost identity and reflect a general recognition that there is in the West a 'crisis in masculinity,' manifested not least through signs of psychological, social and even physical dis-ease.[1] Our present experience of masculinity is widely regarded as being marked by brokenness, so much so that an *Observer* columnist has remarked, 'Men are being treated without the respect due to them as human beings with a distinctive contribution to make to society.'[2]

At the same time, the poor ratio of men to women in many of our churches reveals another side to the 'lostness' of the male gender. Christianity—started by a man, spread by men, founded on texts written almost exclusively by men, its theological history dominated by men, and its leadership comprised, until recently, by men—is, in our culture, at this time, seen as 'feminine,' and seems to provide few real answers to the wider sense of lost identity and purpose affecting men. In an attempt to bridge the gap between men and the church, much work has been done on how evangelism can be made *culturally accessible* for men—more sports evenings, pub quizzes and so on.

This is important work, but there is another equally important avenue to be explored—what, if anything, makes men 'tick' spiritually, *as men*. The writing of this booklet has been driven by the conviction that whatever evangelistic techniques or 'repackaging' we might choose to employ, moving forward will be impossible unless the culture and spirituality of the church is itself renewed. Before we can understand why men outside the church feel alienated from its life and its God, we need to be addressing the more fundamental issues which concern the men already inside the church, the issues which may have more to do with crucial questions of male identity. We must recognize that the lack of men in our churches is not rooted in pathological allergies to the religious or to styles of worship, but perhaps more in our

---

1   For example, James Nelson catalogues a number of ways in which the health of men in the United States is of a far lower standard than that of women. J Nelson, *The Intimate Connection* (London: SPCK, 1992) pp 12–13.
2   Melanie Phillips, *The Observer*, 2nd November, 1997.

own limited understanding of an incarnated faith. We need to explore the roots of where the feminine 'bias' of the church population lies, and to investigate the distinctive features of male identity and masculine spirituality.

There are two sides to the issue. We owe to women and feminist studies a new awareness that gender differences can seriously be explored and celebrated at all. But it has been very difficult for men to find both the 'vocabulary' to talk about what 'masculine spirituality' might mean, and the secure environment in which to do this. We need a framework from which men can

- *affirm the God-given characteristics* of the male gender in the first place, and
- *find starting points* on which to base our sense of specific identity, our ways of relating to God and creation.

The other side of the problem is that men are not starting with a blank sheet. There is the legacy of the past which has already moulded men into certain models of behaviour, both spiritual and otherwise. Our history, theology, worship and practice of life together has been gendered in such a way that we have both institutionalized traditional models of masculinity, while at the same time denying men the opportunity to celebrate the fullness of being male in body, and masculine in mind and spirit. Thus part of the task we face in discovering a way forward for men is to critique the painful past.

On a positive front, there are basic principles of masculine spirituality that I will put forward, and which have arisen from the growth in men's literature in the last decade or so. In particular, exploring the link between sexuality and spirituality, seeking to understand the significance of role models appropriately, and the task of finding metaphors for living as men can offer new and positive direction. It is my belief that there are many untried and exciting ways in which the 'lost male' can be found—for himself and for God. However, it is also true that male identity cannot be discovered in isolation from female identity, and true growth will involve men in dialogue with women about themselves which may at times be painful.

But if we can do this, if we can stretch the boundaries, if we can be liberated from restrictive roles, then Christian men will not only find ways of growing in faith, but the church will also have a lot to offer those men outside the Christian community. Books and films such as *American Beauty, Fight Club, High Fidelity,* and *The Full Monty* reveal a widespread acknowledgement of a sense of 'crisis in masculinity' which pervades Western society. Our culture calls out for a new sense of identity, and an affirmation of what being a man means, which for once is not created by reaction against the feminine, or by a regression to old patterns of behaviour. We need to know and experience in the church, that gender, *masculinity,* is a God-given gift, with the potential to be nurtured, redeemed and celebrated.

2
'Guys are in Trouble'

If men are going to experience healing to any degree, then a thorough diagnosis of the problems faced is the starting point. The Women's movement has paradoxically thrown a lifeline to men—it has acted as spur for men's self-examination, personally and collectively. As a result, men are realizing that inherited gender roles can be just as imprisoning for men as for women. Back in 1978, men were arguing that 'our power in society as men not only oppresses women but imprisons us in a deadening masculinity which cripples all our relationships—with each other, with women, with ourselves.'[3] At the same time, the loss of traditional roles in society has cut away so many anchors for men that there is no longer any secure ground that can be called 'male territory.'

Yet while women have successfully been articulating their oppression, men have to deal with the legacy of having been the 'generic being,' 'mankind,' for centuries—and having no concepts by which their role can be defined *as men*. Having never been talked about as a distinct gender, they have effectively been made invisible to themselves, and it is only dissatisfaction and a lack of comfort that is finally making it clear to them that they need to be able to 'see,' and to be seen. Yet all they have is a vague notion that they '…are in trouble. Manhood, once an opportunity for achievement, now seems like a problem to be overcome.'[4] What are the main symptoms and causes of this 'problem'?

Father Hunger
> *'My father never laid a finger on me…Bastard.'* NSPCC poster

In the novel High Fidelity, the main character, a 'nineties man,' longs to be able to talk about 'being a bloke in the twentieth century' with his father.[5] This reflects a notion that in a real sense men need to be taught how to be men. Steve Biddulph even argues that there is a biological need for boys to have several hours' one-to-one male contact every day.[6] But at their time of need, when it seems that they are being 'castrated by the culture,' Richard Rohr states that 'no one has given us the energy…fathered us, authored us, created us, believed in us in a way to allow us to believe in ourselves.'[7] Thus

---

3   *Achilles Heel*, 1978, quoted in M Pryce, *Finding a Voice* (London: SCM, 1996) p 43.
4   Garrison Keillor, *The Book of Guys*.
5   N Hornby, *High Fidelity* (London: Indigo, 1996) p 102.
6   S Biddulph, *Manhood* (Hawthorn, Stroud, 1994) p 113.
7   Fr R Rohr, *A Man's Approach to God*, Lee Abbey tapes

the root of men's wounds lies in the experience of the absence of a father.

To illustrate the reality of this absence, Steve Biddulph tells a story of how in the mid-1970s the Mattel toy company tried to market a family of dolls called 'The Heart Family.' In trials, however, numerous children removed the 'father doll' from the family. When they were asked why they were not playing with him, they replied, 'He's at work.'[8] Patterns of life and work formed by the Industrial Revolution can be blamed for a breakdown of the relationship between children and fathers, for a situation in which, as fathers' work is removed from the family environment, intimacy becomes replaced by suspicion, mistrust, and finally disillusionment. Knowledge of the father is received second-hand through mothers, and the ideal of the old wise man, who will guide men through, is usurped by a society which would rather idolize twenty-year-olds.

Father hunger can thus produce a lack of motivation and power in men to be creative or life-giving at any deep level. Especially in their emotional life or in the domestic arena they become passive rather than active. Fr Richard Rohr illustrates this point through the story of the man with the withered right hand, who lacked the energy to do anything but react socially to the initiative of others.[9] But father hunger also forces men towards a 'hegemonic masculinity,' where only one set of values can be embraced, those of the dominant male stereotype in Western society.

In contrast to women who form their identities by a continuing attachment to their mothers, as men approach adulthood, they are characterized by the need for separation from the maternal, to be defined as 'other.'[10] At this point, the lack of the father forces men to turn towards other influences as guiding models, abstract images reinforced by the media. But these 'modes of life available to men—the "Rites of Man" being war, work, and sex—only serve to impoverish, delude and alienate them. The harm done to men in and through these structures distorts their relationship with women and with one another.'[11] P Culbertson suggests that concentration of masculinity in these areas has led to four marks of the American (Western) male: penis pride, rugged self-sacrificing independence, professional success and status, and a mixture of sexual activity with women and a pathological homophobia.[12]

Men and Relationships

The difficulties attached to the task of 'separation' are only compounded by the values outlined above—from all quarters men seem required to exercise emotional self-sufficiency. It is interesting that in the UK the poem voted

8   S Biddulph, *Manhood* (Hawthorn, Stroud, 1994) p 111.
9   Fr R Rohr, *A Man's Approach to God*, Lee Abbey tapes.
10   S Biddulph, *ibid*.
11   M Pryce, *Finding a Voice* (London: SCM, 1996) p 68.
12   P Culbertson, *New Adam—The Future of Male Spirituality* (Minneapolis: Fortress Press, 1992) p 23.

nation's favourite in 1996, Kipling's 'If,' echoes these sentiments: 'If you can keep your head when all around you are losing theirs…Then you will be a man, my son!' Yet this way of 'being a man' leads to a fear of failure and vulnerability. James Nelson compares men's 'castration anxiety' with its modern equivalent: 'performance anxiety': only success will provide wholeness![13] The result of this is that man (who is not anatomically accommodating) finds it hard to accommodate 'messy' intimate relationships.[14]

Just as circumstances must be continually manipulated in order to ensure success, so boundaries in relationships are negotiated so as to guard against vulnerability and need. The main character in *High Fidelity* has all possibilities covered:

> 'Everything that's ever gone wrong for me could have been rescued by the wave of a bank manager's wand…or by some quality—determination, self-awareness, resilience—that I might have found within myself, if I'd looked hard enough…If people have to die, I don't want them dying near me. My mum and dad won't die near me, I've made bloody sure of that. When they go, I'll hardly feel a thing.'[15]

A growing awareness of death poses a great threat to the Western male, and the male 'mid-life crisis' can be interpreted as a running away from its growing reality. Men can increasingly withdraw from intimate involvement in family life, perpetuating the cycle of the absent father, and adopting a 'positional,' rather than a personal role.[16] In the inner cities especially, men can eventually find themselves being driven to the edge of communities, as well as of families, as society conspires to continue this pattern. A vicar from an inner-city parish in Bristol notes:

> 'There will be occasions when [men] don't really know where they fit in families—that they are not really welcomed, and that women would rather be on their own than risk sharing their children and their families with men. And therefore there's quite a model now of men being on the edge of family life rather than at the centre of it.'[17]

There is a danger that not expressing intimacy or emotion will lead to not experiencing it. This will lead to less insight, less awareness of one's inner self and a self-destructive failure to recognise that things are going wrong.

However, it also seems that for the majority this is not the case, that such

13 J Nelson, *The Intimate Connection* (London: SPCK, 1992) p 34.
14 P Culbertson, *New Adam—The Future of Male Spirituality* (Minneapolis: Fortress Press,1992) p 17.
15 N Hornby, *High Fidelity* (London: Indigo, 1996) p 184.
16 R Bowl, *Changing the Nature of Masculinity*, Social Work Monograph, (Norwich: UEA, 1985) p 19.
17 From an interview with Rev Will Donaldson, 25th March, 1998.

emotional poverty now 'has to be worked at.'[18] Men and women in the church can rejoice at cracks in the armour of 'masculine hegemony.' The crisis can be an opportunity. We can see '…the current fashion for male loutishness, for *Men Behaving Badly*, as a desperate cry for help—hopefully female help— from a drowning gender.'[19] Christians must explore and model manhood in order to find a place where masculinity and intimacy are not bought at the expense of each other, but are combined. It is here that hope lies for men, both inside and outside the church.

3

Putting Gender in its Place

Gender on the Agenda?

But the first task for the church is perhaps to realize there is an issue at all. When, for example, was the last time you heard a sermon on the gift of gendered identity? Despite the evidence of the imbalance of men and women in church attendance statistics, and anecdotal examples a-plenty, many in the churches seem to be unsure as to whether the issue of gender bears any relevance to Christian faith at all. I have heard Galatians 3.28 ('there is no longer male and female in Christ Jesus') being interpreted as ushering in a new era in which the importance of gender differences between men and women is now eradicated. This is perhaps due to a vagueness about what the words sex and gender signify, and the difference between them. It is worth clarifying the terms here:

- *Sex* refers to our *genetic and physiological make-up* which gives us certain reproductive functions.
- *Gender* can be defined as *that which shapes who we are in relation to those around us*. It describes the ways in which socialization moulds us. To speak of gender is to describe certain polarities in who we are, but 'masculine' and 'feminine' are also *imposed qualities*, dictated by the prevailing norms of a particular society, and not *absolute givens*. They are useful as ways of describing realities which perhaps could be replaced with other labels, but engage us in a way no other terms can.[20]

---

18 '…she knows that I'm someone who doesn't really bother, who has friends he hasn't seen for years, who no longer speaks to anybody that he has ever slept with. But she doesn't know how you have to work at that.' N Hornby, *High Fidelity* (London: Indigo, 1996) p 121.
19 Fay Weldon, 'Pity Poor Men' in the *Guardian*. Date unknown.
20 Fr R Rohr, *A Man's Approach to God*, Lee Abbey tapes.

This is why the notion of what gender roles are is constantly changing within society. Perhaps it is this confusing changing pattern of ideas, seemingly driven by social trends rather than, for example, biblical principles, which has encouraged complacency within churches. However, in becoming indifferent to the importance of gender for men, it could be argued that we in the church have simply swallowed the current Western gender myth reflected in our wider society. That myth is that the ideal person is in fact *androgynous*, capable of being both 'masculine' and 'feminine.'

Androgynous Christianity

Gender theory has offered various interpretations this century, but the concept of androgyny came to the fore in the 1970s. Androgyny celebrates the idea that the sexes are in principle identical in all characteristics and capabilities. Fashionable and seen as politically correct, in its fullest form it concludes that one person alone can achieve 'human potential,' and has led to the idea of 'genderless models of marriage and parenting.'[21] Men and women can manage without each other.

I believe that there is, too, a form of Christian androgyny which is rooted in many of our churches, and which militates against the importance of gender exploration. Many Christians would want to affirm that both masculinity and femininity somehow reflect the multi-faceted nature of God, and have something to do with the fact that he(!) is a God 'in relationship.' God's interrelatedness is revealed in the way that human beings have been made to relate to each other as different kind of beings. But, at the same time, the common misconception of there being neither 'male nor female' in Christ Jesus,[22] leads to a perception that the ultimate aim for Christians, realized after death, is to become Christlike by being disembodied selves, without any gender distinction. Embodied gender is seen as a stepping stone to be discarded on the way to a greater transcendent end. The 'ideal' Christian is therefore androgynous. I began to wonder whether this was the impression I was giving to a large group of mainly 'unchurched' men at a funeral recently, as I stood at the front in a cassock and surplice. The effect of clerical robes seems aimed at disguising both masculinity and femininity.

There is a sense in which men and women can embrace the creative potential of the other's gender identity, to be 'masculine in a womanly way, and feminine in a manly way.'[23] But the language of androgyny reminds us that men and women must neither lose their distinctiveness in seeking to

---

21   Melanie Phillips in *The Observer*, 2nd November, 1997. She attributes much of the current 'crisis in masculinity' to this notion.

22   As Colin Brown points out, the distinction in this passage is not one of function, but of status before God. C Brown (ed), *The New International Dictionary of New Testament Theology* (Carlisle: Paternoster, 1986) p 570.

23   R Rohr and J Martos, *The Wild Man's Journey* (Cincinnati: St Anthony Messenger Press, 1992) p 16.

become genderless, nor must they see gender roles as cast in stone, cages in which we are imprisoned. Rather, there is a middle course to be found where gender roles can be malleable symbols through which we can enrich each other's masculinity or femininity.[24]

If men are to be able to seek a distinctive spiritual identity at all, as a starting point` the Christian community must firmly believe that the image of God can come to its fruition only in a community where we are united yet different, male or female. We need to understand as a church that gender differentiation is created, not accidental.

The key biblical foundation for this can be found in Genesis 1.27. Proponents of androgyny have argued that in Genesis when God created man, *'Male and female* he created *him.'* Separate identity is interpreted as unnecessary. But it is important to go on and to note that the plural is also used to distinguish between male and female in this verse: 'male and female he created *them.'* This deliberate balance clearly reveals God's intention for humanity to be united, but it also emphasizes the blessing of man and woman as beings *distinct* from each other. Both male and female are equal bearers of the divine image.

Gender and the Life of God's Kingdom

The temptation to embrace so-called 'androgynous self-sufficiency' must therefore be resisted by Christians. Instead, it is time to affirm that to be masculine *or* feminine is to be fully human, that our gender is one of *two ways* in which God enables us to embrace life in all its abundance. And yet, paradoxically, because we always experience our own gender in relationship, gender is a gift which reminds men and women that we remain incomplete without each other.

As Christians, we are charged with the building of a kingdom, and some may see gender issues as being secondary to this greater role. Yet this is a false separation. In the life of the kingdom, the complementarity of our roles remains an important factor. Indeed, the redemption of this relationship is part of God's plan of salvation, not superfluous to it. To say that the development of the gender wholeness of man and woman should be set aside in pursuit of the greater role of kingdom builder is flawed. It 'forgets that God's kingdom includes the restoration of creational *shalom* between men and women, as well as the proclamation of God's salvation in Christ.'[25]

So using the primacy of the kingdom as an excuse for maintaining the status quo, particularly in terms of justice in the relationship between the sexes, is self-contradictory. Nevertheless, in describing the place of gender within the Christian life, Mary van Leeuwen presents a helpful analogy of

---

24 See M S van Leeuwen, *Gender and Grace* (Leicester: IVP, 1990) p 70.
25 *ibid*, p 72.

discipleship '…as a series of "offices" or vocations that nest inside each other like the progressively smaller boxes of a child's stacking toy.' The largest box, which overrides the others, is that of the redeemed sinner, committed to building God's kingdom of justice and peace as a member of Christ's body. In the same way that marriage, singleness and parenthood can all be seen to be vocations within God's created order, but, compared to the goals of the kingdom, are not of supreme importance, so too gender roles have an authentic place as *part* of the framework of existence.[26]

The task is to see the importance of giving men the rationale and, if you like, even the *permission* to explore gender identity. In their search for liberation and conversion to a fuller humanity, men must feel free to find the language to describe their own experience. They must believe that it is a valid exercise.

Where Do We Begin To Talk About 'Masculinity'?

The tasks of building bridges between men and God, and of addressing the more general issues of identity crisis among men are intimately connected. If we are to make headway, one of the fundamental needs is for a theology that will be the foundation on which Christians can start to redeem broken masculinity. But before we can begin addressing the question of how to go about this, we need to decide exactly what it is that is in need of redemption. What are we aiming for? What, in fact, are the marks of masculinity? The problem we face is that gender identity is difficult to pin down. For example, there may be more difference between two given men than between one particular man and one woman. Speaking about men's approach to conversion, one vicar notes in two individuals completely different approaches to finding faith:

> 'In two men I've known there is a spectrum. In one there is a man who has said, "I have found my emotional needs being met, and therefore that draws me in to the family, the belonging I didn't have," but another has said, "I like what I see, but is it really true?" And that was the crucial thing.'[27]

If it is hard to generalize about two men in the *same* cultural context, then the issue of what masculinity might signify *across* cultures makes the possibility of progress even more of a challenge. Where then do we start?

---

26 *ibid*.
27 Interview with Rev Will Donaldson, Easton Christian Family Centre, 25th March, 1998.

Two Avenues of Exploration

The debate about how human identity is formed has often been characterized by the contrast between nature and nurture. Is our identity as human beings imprinted upon us through our genes, or is it formed by the circumstances in which we grow up? In the thinking around gender identity the terms of reference are very similar. There are currently two strands of thought in men's studies which offer a way forward: *constructionism*, in which gender identity is seen as something which is in a permanent process of being built; and *essentialism*, in which blueprints of identity which are rooted somewhere deep within men are there to be discovered. I believe a Christian approach should be able to draw from the wisdom of both.

a) Building Masculinity

Many would see society today as being 'reflexive'—whatever norms we might have in terms of behaviour and identity are continually being cross-questioned, as we re-examine our past, respond to the present, and predict what we need to be in the future. There is little sense that anything can be fixed or tied down. In this context, many see the idea of the 'self' as a continuously evolving interplay between different social and cultural forces. It cannot be pinned down, it is 'a project carried on amidst a profusion of reflexive resources: therapy and self-help manuals of all kinds, television programmes and magazine articles.'[28] In this context, the *constructionist*, or building approach to gender sees masculinity as having no single and consistent set of attributes and essence. It may be rooted to some degree in our physical characteristics, but it is much more a product of changing relationships between men and women, history and culture. Constructionists speak of identity as a series of developing *gender projects.*

For Christians, this resonates with the concept of being new creations, in that it offers hope for a reconstructed sense of self, not only in relation to human structures, but fundamentally in relation to God. Through this process of reconstruction, personal and social are inextricably entwined, and any change is not aiming to be merely therapeutic, but will result in improved external relationships.

b) Discovering Masculinity

By contrast *essentialists* believe that real change occurs when men become reunited with an essential masculinity that is within all men, a subconscious blueprint.[29] Writers such as Robert Bly and Richard Rohr appeal to 'arche-

---

28 Anthony Giddens, quoted in M Pryce, *Finding a Voice* (London: SCM, 1996) p 44.
29 'It is our experience that deep within every man there are blueprints, what we can also call "hard wiring" for the calm and positive mature masculine…instinctual patterns and energy configurations probably inherited genetically throughout the generations of our species.' Moore and Gillette in S Weber, *Tender Warrior—God's Design for Men* (Amersham: Scripture Press, 1995) p 40.

types of being' rooted in men. Solutions can be found in the work of the mythopoeic writings of Jungian analysts, who appeal to the rediscovery of the 'deep masculine' through story and myth. Nevertheless, even for those trying to discover the 'essence of masculinity,' the patterns of manhood suggested remain 'intrinsically plural...mixed, complex, ambiguous.'[30]

The Christian Gender Project

Men need to find new purposes, new vision, and new identity. Both constructionists and essentialists are trying to do this. They are seeking an expression that will give a voice to men, and break 'the silence of an undeveloped or lost language.' But the task of trying to understand what it is to be a man by taking account both of the social and cultural influences which form us *and* by affirming that our masculinity is also somehow grounded in our bodies and minds is difficult and elusive. Christians need a both/and approach, which affirms that there are essentialist truths about identity, but also that our identities are multidimensional. We should not be afraid of seeking to construct an identity for men which meets them where they are now—socially and culturally—and provides a way forward for an encounter with God and growth in their understanding of themselves as males made in God's image. Any groping towards this will be provisional, but will also find markers and archetypes which point to a reality embracing unity and diversity in a gendered humanity. As Christians, we can embrace the insights of essentialism and the power of images as providing inspiration along the way, rather than as being the final destination of our search.

---

30 M Pryce, *Finding a Voice* (London: SCM, 1996) p 63.

4
'Masculine Spirituality'

If we accept in principle that the need exists for men to articulate their identity, to once again be affirmed in their gender, and to seek ways of knowing God as men, what are the paths along which they might make such a journey? This chapter outlines principles from which reconstructed masculine spirituality might be sought, and the following chapter will try and spell out more practical ways in which such an exercise may be nurtured within the church.

Reuniting Spirit and Body

'The Word, in order to touch me, must become warm flesh. Only then do I understand—when I can smell, see and touch.'[31]

The Jesuit writer Richard Rohr argues that for too long the church has been 'swirling in the *false feminine*…and is characterized by too much inwardness, preoccupation with relationships, a morass of unclarified feeling and endless self-protectiveness.'[32] What does he mean? In the classic Myers-Briggs formula men are portrayed as being Extrovert, Sensate, Thinking, and Judging—reality is 'out there.' Women on the other hand are Introvert, Intuitive, Feeling and Perceiving. With its emphasis on 'personal relationship,' 'private devotion,' 'life in the spirit' and 'feeling close to God,' Christian spirituality today often appeals more to the latter characteristics than the former. This can be seen in the majority of new worship songs in the last twenty years. A few phrases from well-known choruses illustrate the point: 'When I look into your holiness, / When I gaze into your loveliness…', 'When I feel the touch / Of your hand upon my life…', 'O Lord, you're beautiful, / Your face is all I seek…'[33] There is nothing wrong with these sentiments in themselves, and this is certainly a selective sample, but it represents a trend.

Christian activity seems to be understood as occurring mostly in the realms of the 'spirit' or 'soul,' traditionally a female domain. But in a study *Women's ways of knowing: the development of Self, Voice and Mind*, quoted by James Ashbrook,[34] the authors claim that men tend not to trust an approach to life which relies on intuition and experiential knowledge, believing that '…an experiential approach to knowledge easily falls into the trap of subjectivity.

---

31   N Kazantzakis in J Nelson, *The Intimate Connection* (London: SPCK, 1992) p 118.
32   R Rohr and J Martos, *The Wild Man's Journey* (Cincinnati: St Anthony Messenger Press, 1992) p 222.
33   Written respectively by Wayne and Cathy Perrin; Keri Jones and David Matthews; Keith Green, in *Songs of Fellowship* (Eastbourne: Kingsway, 1991).
34   James B Ashbrook in Thatcher (ed), *Christian Perspectives on Sexuality and Gender* (Leominster: Gracewing, 1996) p 98.

As a check, therefore, men approach issues as objectively as possible. In contrast, many women prize experience.' A spirituality rooted in inward subjective truth is harder for men to grasp.

Men also see mystery as *external* to them—something to be penetrated and explored, not to be subjectively nurtured within.[35] Men can be frustrated by things which cannot be touched, seen, heard, judged. The task for the church is thus to recover the Jewish sense of the self as unifying mind, spirit *and* body in a spirituality which can make sense of this physical life. Judaism includes a *berakhah* (blessing) upon leaving the toilet, and thanking God for creating us with orifices by which things go in and come out.[36] So it is ironic that in the most incarnational of faiths we have required physical experience to be 'spiritualized.' But there 'is a growing sense that theology must be grounded in this kind of experiential stuff. If we do not know the gospel in our bodies, perhaps we do not know it.'[37]

Men need to be encouraged to know God in their pain, their creativity, their sexuality, their youth, their taste in music, their ageing, their response to the created world. The resurrection of the body affirms the place of physical pleasure, and perhaps in this area the church has most to give men. For men who run from the vulnerability death brings, resurrection enables them to be at home in this life because they know death is not the end.

Discovering Wholeness in the Polarity of Sexuality

In finding a way forward for men, a rediscovery of the biblical vision of the whole person who is not split into a higher spirit and a lower flesh is crucial. James Nelson's vision of the 'intimate connection' between sexuality and spirituality cuts a path beyond androgyny towards a wholeness for men as men. In affirming the body and sexuality, men can begin to see within their own bodies the capacity for spiritual growth. Anatomy is not destiny, but there is a complex and important relationship between anatomy and spirituality—we are our bodies, we do not have them. What makes men anatomically male can provide clues for their spiritual identity.

Nelson explores the experience of men's sexuality as a way into masculine spirituality. What he calls 'phallic strength'—found in the state of erection—provides the first clue. This strength can be affirmed as essential for a healthy masculinity, for 'without its integrated positive energy, man lacks direction and movement...the urge to extend himself from the mediocre.'[38] He also points out, however, that 'phallus' in our society has perhaps been replaced by 'priapism,' which lives in fear of deflation.

35 *ibid*, p 35.
36 P Culbertson, *New Adam—The Future of Male Spirituality* (Minneapolis: Fortress Press, 1992) p 122.
37 J Nelson, *The Intimate Connection* (London: SPCK, 1992) p 115. He is talking here of physical, external experience.
38 Nelson, *ibid*, p 92.

15

Patriarchy and machismo relies upon this 'phallic state' being permanent. However, the picture changes if we think of the opposite of erection not as being deflation, but *relaxation*. Men need not idolize phallic power, not because they are to be ashamed of it, nor because the phallus is something to be embarrassed about, but because it gives a false sense of what God values in them. God values men as whole people, not just when they are standing in their 'phallic strength.'

Nelson argues that men's sense of wholeness will be found in understanding that which is their main awareness for the majority of the time—penis. He writes, 'The penis, contrary to the phallus, is a creature of the dark...But without the darkness there is no growth, no mystery, no receptivity, no deep creativity...Without the gentle dark, light becomes harsh.'[39] It is in the soft vulnerability and weakness of this state that men can move away from the values by which they are entrapped. Men's identity is to be found not in one state or the other but in both. In the polarity of penis and phallus men can be freed to explore the whole range of their emotional structure—a development which is vital for prayer and worship—activities which demand a whole sweep of emotions:

> 'The hard and explosive phallic achievement becomes in an instant the soft vulnerable tears of the penis. Both are fully male. Both are deeply grounded in a man's bodily reality. Both dimensions of life are fully present when a man is most human.'[40]

The Role of 'Masculine Archetypes'

This idea of a polarity in masculine spirituality has also been expressed through metaphors which seek to provide archetypes or blueprints for discovering a fuller male identity. For example, John Bell of the Iona Community has reflected on how the words describing Jesus as the 'Lamb of God' have different meanings in the New Testament. *Amnos* in the Gospel of John portrays Jesus as the vulnerable, innocent victim, while *arneon* in the Revelation of John refers to the Lamb as leader of the pack, a pioneer in areas of great risk.[41] Similarly, Richard Rohr uses John the Baptist and John the Beloved as revealing two ends of a spectrum in masculinity, corresponding to the 'deep masculine' and the 'common feminine.'[42] The latter is provoked by a meaningful interaction with women. These metaphors can provide useful frameworks through which men can explore the fullness of their identity.

But if, as Roy McCloughry suggests, the journey of faith is that of moving from being a Christian to becoming Christlike,[43] in what sense can Jesus serve as the ultimate archetype for men as men? What clues can be found in him

---

39 *ibid*, p 96.
40 *ibid*, p 111.
41 John Bell, *Men Only*, Greenbelt tapes.
42 Fr R Rohr, *A Man's Approach to God*, Lee Abbey tapes.

towards a more authentic masculinity? If Jesus is to have any meaning for men, we must affirm his maleness as a significant part of his humanity, while acknowledging that his humanity remains the important factor. We perhaps need to emphasize more the fact that Jesus was a man, as well as being God. The traditional approach, as demonstrated in most (though not all) artists' portrayals of Jesus, has been to seek to emasculate Jesus in an attempt to find a divinely androgynous ideal. This has led to common misconceptions, by Bly and others, of Jesus as a 'blessed' but anti-erotic model of manhood.[44]

Indeed, God could be said to be exercising a gender bias towards the 'weaker sex' by sending Jesus as a man! Only by being a man could Jesus be in a position to undermine in his humanity the fractured, power-hungry and distorted masculinity that existed and continues to exist. He gives up the ultimate male power, allowing himself to be helped by a woman, and embracing pain and the vulnerability of death.[45]

Thus through his incarnation Jesus has two messages for men trapped in masculinity. He affirms their bodies, but also gives a message that they can be set free from conventional masculinity. He is simultaneously 'a compelling picture of male sexual wholeness, of creative masculinity, and of the redemption of manhood from both oppressiveness and superficiality.'[46]

But Jesus must not be seen only in this light. There is a danger that in adopting him as a 'manly model,' Christians may turn him into either an unreachable ideal, or into 'the triumph of male power.' Preaching Jesus as the ultimate 'man's man' may stir the heartstrings, but perpetuates the idea of salvation as a man's project, where success or failure become the criteria. In contrast, Jesus offers wholeness based on the power of love, a much more life-giving reality than ideas of male domination can provide.

Reaching Out—The Problem of Passivity

We now shift our focus a little away from those who perhaps have an established Christian faith, and more towards those who may be new Christians or simply on the fringe of the church community with no faith commitment at all. Here, a search for spirituality and evangelistic concerns coincide. Traditional evangelistic approaches to men have focused on a three-pronged strategy of providing interesting incentives to get men to a place where we can hear the gospel, preaching a message which emphasizes their need for forgiveness and salvation, to which they must respond by becoming passive and receptive, and then calling them onwards into commitment (active). If we put this in Nelson's terms, in order to become Christians, men are to embrace the reality of 'penis' before that of 'phallus,' or in Rohr's, to make

---

43 R McCloughry, *Men without Masks* (Grove Pastoral Booklet, P 59) p 9.
44 M Pryce, *Finding a Voice* (London: SCM, 1996) p 63.
45 *ibid*.
46 *ibid*, p 103.

the journey of 'John the Beloved' before that of 'John the Baptist.'

There is nothing wrong with any of these ideas in themselves, but my suspicion is that for a lot of men, the journey from 'power to love,' or from 'strength to vulnerability' or from 'self to other/God' cannot be made through passive recognition of need in what could be described as the 'intuitive/feminine' consciousness. The journey that men are often asked to make will only happen once they have 'decided to learn,' and have begun to be comfortable in a context where they can share their own stories. Perhaps alternative routes, which enable men to reach such a position, can be found.

Creative Purpose and Adventure

'…in a survey, 60% of women said that need or crisis precipitated their encounter with God. The self-sufficient male will not find this his experience. Rather, he needs to know where *he fits in with God's plan.*'[47]

Richard Rohr laments the fact that 'in today's culture men's energies are hardly directed towards the creation of life and the production of real things.'[48] Yet, as we have seen, there is a need in men to extend themselves; part of their identity as men is revealed by the way they are anatomically designed to create. For Rohr, a part of masculine fulfilment is 'oriented toward work, task, and accomplishment,' and balanced masculinity 'shows itself in action undertaken for the sake of others.'[49] Similarly, other writers see the highest masculine impulse as being 'willed to a Higher creative impulse.'[50] While I would wish to assert that the need to be active and productive *contributes partly* to masculine identity, rather than being its *fulfilment*, it nevertheless may be this insight that holds the key for the church's reaching out to men.

As we have seen, many men are suffering from a profound loss of identity and purpose. Thus, rather than waiting for men to passively accept the gospel, conversion (as an initial and ongoing process) may well come better in the context of active involvement in the community of faith, where in giving, men reach a place where they can receive. They *become wedded to a Higher Purpose in the process of serving it.* They don the mantle of John the Baptist before that of John the Beloved. Rev Chris Sunderland's experience of working in an inner-city parish seems to back this up:

'Most men round here aren't interested in the ideas the church has, but they will get involved, particularly with the practical stuff. They like to be part of the community…That's the approach I take with them.'[51]

This approach is deductive in the sense that it sees *circumstances and experi-*

---

47   Derek Cook, *We Are His Witnesses* (Cumbria: Maranatha, 1996).
48   R Rohr and J Martos, *The Wild Man's Journey* (Cincinnati: St Anthony Messenger Press, 1992) p 65.
49   *ibid*, pp 126–9.
50   John Gaynor Banks, quoted in L Payne, *Crisis in Masculinity* (Eastbourne: Kingsway, 1985) p 44.
51   From an interview, April, 1998.

ence as being more important than *ideas* in conversion. Richard Rohr states that in putting ourselves into new situations we can find our viewpoint being changed.[52] Action and reflection are symbiotic in the Christian life. Men outside the church need to be engaged in the former before they can be led into the latter. The question we therefore need to be asking about men is not so much 'How can they hear?' as 'How can they become involved so that they might learn?'

However, in seeking to call men by awakening a healthy sense of vocation, there are dangers to be avoided. I would suggest the metaphors of adventure and journeying, in which the destination is something other than our own development, provide a better language than that of the recent notion of being a 'Promise Keeper.' It seems to me that this language adopts criteria of success and failure, where failure is the certain outcome. There is a danger that spirituality is turned into a project, a game of merit and demerit, in which we are being watched to see how we are measuring up.[53] Some commentators have seen in the 'Promise Keepers' a replaying of patriarchal Christianity (in that it fails to ask men to lay down power)[54] and the perpetuation of a fundamentalism which translates the redundant Western values of masculinity into Christian terms.

Whole Life Christianity

A persistent attempt to counteract the dualistic view that permeates much of 'church life' (a phrase which, in itself, stems from dualism), and a consequent living out of our discipleship in every area of life will persuade men that Christ is relevant to their bodily, physical, concrete reality. We have much to learn from the integral perspective of the reformational worldview, which does not accept a distinction between sacred and secular realms in the cosmos.[55] Rather, a recognition that we are called to participate in the ongoing creational work of God will enable the church to be much more open to the positive possibilities for service to God in areas of life which concern working men. As one vicar has said, 'It's difficult for men to realize that their ability to earn money and provide for their families is a gift from God.'[56] If we are unable to affirm this ourselves, then men will never be able to see the church as belonging to anything else except another, more feminine, world.

---

52 Fr R Rohr, *A Man's Approach to God*, Lee Abbey tapes.
53 'It is about being totally unrelaxed in the presence of God because God is judging every fibre of our being and every thought in our brain 24 hours a day.' John Bell, *Third Way*, October 1996. I doubt whether this was the original intention of 'Promise Keepers' at all, but the language we use can too easily influence our choices and patterns of behaviour.
54 'Promise Keepers assert a necessary connection between a patriarchal reading of Christianity and authentic manhood.' Mark W Muesse quoted in S Boyd (ed), *Redeeming Men—Religion and Masculinities* (Louisville: Westminster John Knox, 1996) p 85.
55 A Wolters, *Creation Regained* (Leicester: IVP, 1986) p 10.
56 Rev Will Donaldson, 25th March, 1998.

5
Ways Ahead

The growth of men's groups in recent years has been the forum where thinking, searching and praying through some of these issues has been done, and such groups will undoubtedly provide the best context in which some of the ideas raised here may be explored. I would now like to suggest other ways in which the life of an individual church could and should be further developed to enable this process to continue.

Regendering the Church

An insight from the constructionist approach is that 'masculinity and femininity are inherently relational concepts...as an object of knowledge masculinity is always masculinity-in-relation.'[57] It follows that an essential stage on the journey towards masculinity must be a renegotiation of men's relationship with women, as it has been formed by the tide of history. For many feminists, the essentialist approach, however well intentioned, fails to address the legacy of patriarchy in society and in the church. Despite the danger of generalizations, anthropologists agree that one constant factor across societies is oppression of women by men.

If there is to be real progress for men and women, men must see that the private self is not something untainted by the legacy of the past, but that it has been partly formed by power relations in society that have created injustice and distortion. Part of men's journey is to acknowledge and take responsibility for why things are as they are. Thus feminists suggest that it is only women who are able to offer an adequate critique for judging the trustworthiness of any men's movements.

In order to grow then, men must realize that they must let the last vestiges of patriarchy fade away from their relationships and from within their hearts. They can no longer afford to ignore women, without whom their masculinity has no real meaning. They will only be able to find a truly liberating way of being men by looking outside themselves, by making themselves attentive to the needs and voices of women, and changing their life choices in response. This will mean letting go of coercive, abusive and dominating behaviour—a change that may only happen through a conscious effort. This process will involve men and women listening to each other's stories, hurts and fears, trying to understand the history of the social power relationships that have caused alienation between the genders, and finally

---

[57]   M Pryce, *Finding a Voice* (London: SCM, 1996) p 78.

grieving and repenting together. Being drawn together in the community of faith faces us with this challenge, but also lends us the opportunity. Church and family can be the place where this agenda is consciously pursued. John Bell puts it in this way:

'...we have to establish a relationship of mutuality in which men do not surrender authority to women and then feel hurt or ashamed at having given away so much but we identify in women the gift, the experience, the perspective, the skill, which when brought into play with our attributes will change us and form a different kind of harmony.'[58]

This harmony can be represented as the word for 'togetherness,' or 'fellowship' in the New Testament—*koinonia*. It describes a pattern of relationship characterized by attachment, rather than separation, reaching out instead of grasping, becoming vulnerable instead of needing to control. Only change in alliance with women will heal men. Through the ordination of women, a growing awareness of the importance of inclusive language, and some creative new liturgy, the church has begun the brave process of recognizing how our theology and practice has been gendered in the past. This regendering needs now to affect every aspect of our lives together, and every facet of our separate identities, and to filter through the day by day relationships of Christians in local communities.

Deciding to Learn

In a sociological study, *Paths to Colleagueship*, Carol Pierce and Bill Page plot out a continuum which charts men and women's behaviour and attitudes as they change from rape and coercion all the way through to being able to integrate masculine and feminine ways of thinking. The central point on this journey is *deciding to learn*. It is only when men have decided to change that they can become increasingly non-protective of themselves. Their insight is that everyone must be got to this point before any other progress can be made.[59] Thus the first job for the church is not only to give men permission to speak, but to encourage them to do so. There must be an active and consistent acknowledgement that this is a necessary task within the church community.

Celebrating Difference

I have previously pointed out the need for men and women to share stories—in being offered opportunities to do so men will begin to grow. But our awareness of ourselves as distinct can be nurtured through worship that

---

58 John Bell in *Third Way*, October 1996.
59 P Culbertson, *New Adam—The Future of Male Spirituality* (Minneapolis: Fortress, 1992) pp 127–8.

helps us to celebrate our diversity, as well as our unity—worship which gives us different, but complementary voices, worship where we do not merely echo one another (in most choruses it is usually the women echoing the men!) or speak in unison, but where we are able to speak encouragement *to* each other. There are some positive signs in this area, notably the liturgy of the Iona Community. The song, 'Shout to the North' is another good example: '*Women*: Men of faith rise up and sing / Of the great and glorious king / You are strong when you feel weak / In your brokenness complete...*Men*: Rise up women of the truth / Stand and sing to broken hearts...'[60]

Modelling Vulnerability

Culbertson argues that the first task for the church 'is to urge men to trust God enough to arrive in God's presence with an open heart.'[61] Men, terrified of failure, need to hear God's voice as the voice of encouragement, which says to men, 'Do not be afraid.'[62] They have to know fundamentally that they are accepted, that they are loved by God in Christ, and are set free from fears of not meeting the father-God's expectations. On their journey they must therefore be allowed to see failure as being success, and be set free from the need for results.

Richard Rohr affirms the value of seeing *gift* as the other side of *wounds*. He uses Bly's analysis of a necessary *katabasis*, or 'ashes experience,' to show how it is only a willingness to accept failure that will lead men to the heart of masculine spirituality—risk taking.[63] For if men are committed to performing before God, or if 'we are perfectionists or purists here we shall find ourselves cut off from all experience of love.'[64] Leaders in the church are in a position to give a lead in risk taking to provide the initial model. It of course demands that they themselves are beginning to walk the same path, however uncomfortable.[65]

Metaphors and Approachable Archetypes

Alongside this, a renewed emphasis in our preaching on the men in the Bible as presenting 'less of an unmeetable challenge—more an invitation to authenticity'[66] will help men to embrace risk-taking and to trust God's love. Mark Pryce has shown how we can view biblical patriarchs either as 'set in stone' or 'formed as flesh.'[67] Can men therefore be encouraged to identify

---

60 Martin Smith, copyright Furious Music, 1994.
61 P Culbertson, *New Adam—The Future of Male Spirituality* (Minneapolis: Fortress Press, 1992) p 143.
62 M Pryce, *Finding a Voice* (London: SCM, 1996) p 31.
63 Fr R Rohr, *A Man's Approach to God*, Lee Abbey tapes.
64 J Nelson, *The Intimate Connection* (London: SPCK, 1992) p 91.
65 'A space-making, question asking, self-disclosing ministry of mutual vulnerability may feel strange, for it is not shaped by one-sided phallic understandings. But it is the sort of ministry that connects people and enhances their size.' *ibid*, p 128.
66 M Pryce, *Finding a Voice* (London: SCM, 1996) p 35.
67 *ibid*, p 37.

with Moses, the man who ran away in fear, as well as Moses the 'Law Giver'? Or to see Paul, the courageous missionary, also as the one who experienced God's grace as sufficient? Can we read the stories in the gospels not just as inspiration for our discipleship, but also as memories of failure and grace? Then there are metaphors drawn from the 'feminine,' for example new birth, little children, the kingdom as yeast in the dough, Jesus as 'mother hen,' God as 'nursing Israel' to name a few, which may lead men into new paradigms, into an understanding that growth and risk are important.

Space to Speak

While interaction with women remains vital, men's groups provide a means to a good end. If we take the idea of masculinity only existing fully in relationship to femininity seriously, then men's groups will never become male-bonding exercises, or self-development groups, but mechanisms to allow men to look outward to better relationships with women. They will enable men to discuss their experience subjectively,[68] rather than having to analyse it objectively.

Deborah Tannen distinguishes between *rapport* talk and *report* talk, as being feminine and masculine tendencies respectively. She thus affirms the way in which men need to be able to interact with each other as men, so as not to feel uncomfortable about their style of sharing. Many men have found such groups to be a context where performance and competition can be left behind, and where articulation of fears and wounds can begin to take place.[69]

Groups can also be places where men can rediscover the missing grace of intimate friendship. Having recognized the problems men have with intimacy, the church must develop an appreciation of friendship between men as not being 'goal' or 'activity' based, but as an arena for learning about passive receptiveness and mutual reciprocity. For if they are unable to ask others for help, how will they be able to ask God?

Story

Allowing men to share subjectively affirms the value of 'bodily, experiential stuff' as being of importance in their relationship with God. 'Theology which doesn't engage with human life is a bit like science which doesn't engage with the natural world,'[70] and perpetuates the dualism which we have seen can alienate men. An inductive approach also affirms that the truth of God is found in 'the depth process of human experience, rather than in the linearity of doctrinal formulas.'[71] This way of 'doing theology' affirms men's lives and identities as they are, and enables them to 'live (their) way

---

68   Sam Keen quoted in J Nelson, *The Intimate Connection* (London: SPCK, 1992) p 51.
69   R McCloughry, *Men and Masculinity* (London: Hodder and Stoughton, 1992) p 122.
70   From an interview with Rev Chris Sunderland, St Luke's, Barton Hill, April 1998.
71   P Culbertson, *New Adam—The Future of Male Spirituality* (Minneapolis: Fortress Press, 1992) p 135.

into a new way of thinking, rather than to think (their) way into a new way of living.' It provides an accessible, unthreatening starting point for growth. 'Most people find it difficult to reflect, to say "This is what I think life is about." Telling stories about their lives is a way in to reflecting on the gospel.'[72] Rather than being asked to articulate a series of beliefs, simply being asked to share experience can be something all men can engage in. God becomes authentically real to them through this liberating testimony, and by being enabled to tell their autobiographies with a new critical awareness, they can recognize where change is necessary.

The Wisdom of Experience

'Never being welcomed into the male world by older men is a wound in the chest.'[73]

The image of the boy Jesus in the temple surrounded by older men speaks to us not only of his advanced wisdom, but also of a society where young men are given a hearing, where their 'growing pains' are cushioned by the affirmation of those who have gone there before. Boys and young men in our day, and especially those whose own fathers may be 'absent,' face a daunting task in learning how to be men. As a final point, therefore, I suggest that we need to explore the untapped resources of age and accumulated wisdom among the older men in our churches. For young men who are perhaps feeling trapped by the conventional and dehumanizing forms of masculinity on offer, developing relationships with older men may provide a way in which they can be nurtured, inspired, and find a place to begin to tell their own unfolding stories. We are looking for men who are able to pass on 'energy, rather than ideas.'[74] This may be a hard task to undertake, and too high an expectation for many. Older men may not feel, or realize, they have anything to give. But for those who can take on such a 'mentoring' role, part of the value of such relationships would not only be a journey away from the alienation of the 'generation gap,' but a step towards what knowing the self, knowing others, and knowing God *as a man* might mean.

---

72 From in interview with Rev Chris Sunderland, St Luke's, Barton Hill, April 1998.
73 R Bly, *Iron John* (Shaftesbury: Element, 1990) p 32.
74 Fr R Rohr, *A Man's Approach to God*, Lee Abbey tapes.